Other NEW YORKER books

The New Yorker Book of Cat Cartoons (1990)

The Complete Book of Covers from *The New Yorker*, 1925—1989 (1989)

THE
NEW YORKER
BOOK OF DOG CARTOONS

THE
NEW YORKER
BOOK OF DOG CARTOONS

ALFRED A. KNOPF NEW YORK 1992

THIS IS A BORZOI BOOK
PUBLISHED BY ALFRED A. KNOPF, INC.

Library of Congress Cataloging-in-Publication Data

The New Yorker book of dog cartoons.— 1st ed.
p. cm.
Includes index.
ISBN 0-679-41680-3
1. Dogs—Caricatures and cartoons. 2. American wit and humor, Pictorial.
3. New Yorker (New York, N.Y.: 1925) I. New Yorker (New York, N.Y.: 1925)
NC1428.N47 1992
741.5'973—dc20   92-70913
CIP

Manufactured in the United States of America

First Edition

THE
NEW YORKER
BOOK OF DOG CARTOONS

"*Hey, the tide has turned!*"

"Mongrels have it up here."

"Shut up, Prince! What's biting you?"

4

"The bidding will start at eleven million dollars."

"Did you woof?"

"*If you had an account here, it would be a different story.*"

"Joe, I want out."

"*Now play dead.*"

"Well, your nose feels cold."

Bernard Schoenbaum.

"You will be going on a long walk."

13

"We think it's a glandular disturbance."

14

IT'S TIME TO TREAT YOUR DOG TO
Le Bon Chien.®
THE FIRST HAMBURGER- FLAVORED LIQUEUR <u>FOR</u> <u>CANINES</u> <u>ONLY</u>!

Try serving Le Bon Chien® in any of these delightful ways:

"Fido."

Fill bowl with ice cubes. Pour 3 oz. Le Bon Chien® over ice. Serve.

"Lassie in Reruns"

Mix 2 cups water with ¼ cup Le Bon Chien® in bowl. Serve.

"101 Dalmatians"

Pour 12 oz. club soda into bowl. Add 3 oz. Le Bon Chien®. Float slice of bologna on top. Serve.

R.Cht

HEEL PAW
STAY LIE
COME JUMP
SIT SIC 'EM
FETCH BEG

Edward Gorey

17

"She's very like her father and has something of his sense of humor."

"Do you want to handle this or should I?"

"Stop fawning!"

"He's about five feet six, has big brown eyes and curly blond hair, and answers to the name of Master."

"*We should get out to the country more often.*"

"Et tu, Baxter?"

"I'm going to disqualify myself."

"She never took to the leash."

"Yes, I'm talking to you. I believe you're
the only Sparky in the house."

"*You remember Trixie, don't you, Freddie?*"

"They never pushed me. If I wanted to retrieve, shake hands, or
roll over, it was entirely up to me."

"We want to send a hostess present to a dachshund."

"If you lie down with pugs, you wake up with pugs."

"*Come here a minute, dear. Skeeter's learned a new trick.*"

"And <u>this</u>, I presume, is Fluffy?"

"*I understand that in your country this thing is done quite differently.*"

"I didn't realize, Your Honor. I assumed the law here
was the same as in New Jersey. As you may know, dog
eat dog is permissible there."

"It's very gratifying, but there's a lot of responsibility
that goes along with it."

"He's been trained in guard duty, attack, and litigation."

"*The father belonged to some people who were driving through in a Packard.*"

"Don't give the dog any more coffee."

BOOTH

"First then: the bulk of my estate, excepting certain specific bequests
as hereinafter noted, I leave to my true friend and companion,
one of God's noblest creatures ..."

STEINBERG

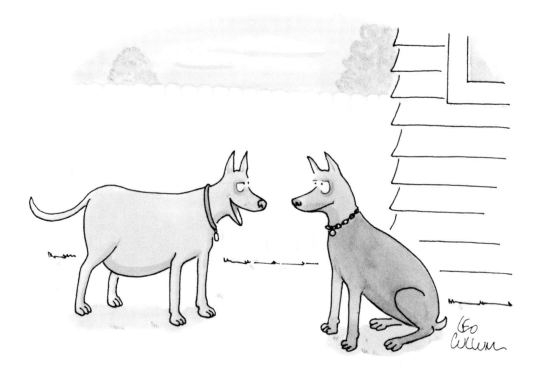

If it's girls, Kimberly, Kaitlin, Lauren, Cindy, and Tracy.
If it's boys, Cameron, Christopher, Adam, Jeffrey, and Gregory."

"*This one's from you know who, so make a fuss and thank him.*"

CHILDREN OF
CELEBRITY CANINES

BRITTANY:

Daughter of Lassie. Hopes to become an actress/model. Not completely without talent, but close.

LANCE:

Benji's offspring. At the moment, wants to be a rock-and-roll drummer. A borderline socio-pathic ne'er-do-well.

SO WHATCHA LOOKIN' AT, HUH?

ROVER:

Son of Andalusian Dog. Happy and well adjusted. Nothing at all like his dad.

R. Chast

"*Under our holistic approach, Mr. Wyndot, we not only treat your symptoms, we also treat your dog.*"

"Well, please look again, Operator. It's Fluffy—
F-L-U-F-F-Y—and she lives in Larchmont."

"*Once again I find myself in the rather awkward position of having to ask one of you for a biscuit.*"

"Do you, Daisy, promise to love, honor, and, in particular, obey Mr. Singer? To beg, sit, stay, heel, and roll over until death do you part?"

"He's *terribly* jealous of Fifi."

"The works."

"*You ought to spend more time with your own species.*"

"It's a shame. He's lost the will to fetch."

O. SOGLOW

"'I'm a good dog, Mama, I'll bring you your daily news.
I'm a good dog, Mama, I don't chew my master's shoes.
But there's one thing life has learnt me—even good dogs get the blues.'
Blow some sweet harp for me, Lucky."

"He's only four weeks old, and he can already say 'arf.'"

"Pray for it."

THE BLOODHOUND AND THE BUG

1

2

3

4

5

6

7

8

9

11

11½

12

13

14

15

Thurber

"He _is_ cute, but you already have a dog."

"Sold!"

"He may be a fine veterinarian, but we're going to get some funny looks."

"*I think the Greeks are running out of ideas.*"

"He's got it! The Frug!"

"...and the balance of my estate I want to put into a trust for the care and maintenance of my most loyal friend and faithful companion, my dog Spot. Now go out and get me a dog with spots."

"Did you or did you not employ a leash to drag your cairn terrier, Jack, away from the corner of Park Avenue and Sixty-fifth Street in spite of his making every effort to clearly indicate to you that he wished to stay where he was?"

"Well, they consider him a member of the family."

"I'll lay it out for you. We're cutting back, and
we no longer need a dog."

"You've got to get rid of one or the other. It's getting on my nerves."

"I've told you why I need a dog. Now suppose you tell me
what makes you think you might be that dog."

"Woof woof woof woof!... I mean, get me the Techcorp file, Thompson."

"You realize I'm taking an enormous personal as well as professional risk just being seen with you."

"It's always 'Sit,' 'Stay,' 'Heel'—never 'Think,' 'Innovate,' 'Be yourself.'"

"From now on, Ted, I will speak only when
adequately represented by counsel."

"We must be in the Italian Alps."

"*And I'm happy to be here, Johnny.*"

"*Are you two looking for trouble, Mister?*"

"Now, look! It says right here on the can how good this is for you:
'Recommended by veterinarians everywhere. Beef livers appetizingly
cooked in their own juices. Vitamin C added. Contains minimum daily
requirement of riboflavin . . .'"

*"If you two are through with your braised sirloin tips, I'll
just go ahead and clear the table."*

"The quick brown dog jumps over the lazy fox."

"*How long have you and Charlie been together?*"

"Speak."

"Heel."

"Roll over."

"Stay."

"*I used to think it was cruel to keep a dog in the city,*
but Homer's made a remarkable adjustment."

"Speaking personally, I haven't had my day, and I've never met any dog who has."

"He has my bite and his father's bark."

Index of Artists

The text of this book was set in a postscript version of Caslon Old Face No. 2
on a Macintosh IIci. Printed and bound by Halliday Lithographers,
West Hanover, Massachusetts.
Designed by Virginia Tan.